THE NEW YORK CITY
MANHATTAN
COLORING BOOK

SECOND EDITION

DRAWINGS BY
DAVID EDWARD BYRD

CONCEIVED & CREATED BY
WILLIAM W. RIPPNER / DAVID EDWARD BYRD

WITH TEXT BY PAUL GOLDBERGER

PRODUCED BY
WILLIAM W. RIPPNER

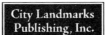

City Landmarks Publishing, Inc.

INTRODUCTION

New Yorkers are often surprised that much of the city they once loved is no longer there. They should not be; change is in the blood of this city, and always has been. A theme running through much of the nineteenth century commentary on the city is the frustration of observers at seeing their favorite places disappear.

Nonetheless, there is a different sense today, perhaps because we pushed things a bit too far in the last two decades and made change more sweeping than either our economics or our emotions necessarily required. So there now is a renewed interest in the city's past—a desire to preserve what we can and, more important, to apply lessons from what is already here to what we build in the future.

A review of 30 structures does not make a book on a city. But the mysteries of Manhattan are such that 300 structures would not be enough either, nor 3,000; for in New York knowing the parts is only a step toward knowing the whole. The whole, if it can be grasped at all, comes slowly, over time, from immersing oneself in the richness of the urban landscape, the ordinary places as well as the extraordinary ones.

But the 30 special places which follow are surely a good place to start.

Paul Goldberger

FOREWORD

"We shape our buildings, and they shape us."
--WINSTON CHURCHILL

This book is a tribute to the architecture of New York City, the frozen music that shapes us all.

THE NEW YORK TIMES MANHATTAN COLORING BOOK was conceived at our first meeting, November 1972. Being incurable romantics about New York City, especially Manhattan and its architecture, we agreed that a book of line drawing with text would be our method of celebrating this magical energy center. It is our belief that architecturally correct line drawings point up the intrinsic beauty and rhythm of the subjects chosen and we hope that other books of line drawing will be created to reflect our rich, varied architectural and cultural heritage.

Perhaps this book will aid the growing movement to preserve and restore the best in our past. Only by recognizing this treasure can we encourage more astute urban planning for the future . . . and a more humane and visually pleasing New York City.

William W. Rippner/David Edward Byrd
April 15, 1975

RADIO CITY MUSIC HALL

is a grand survivor–the only one of the great thirties movie palaces to continue functioning into the present day, and one of the city's few art deco interiors preserved almost intact.

The immense foyer is one of the city's finest interior spaces, and a true monument to art deco. The elegant sweeping staircase, cylindrical chandeliers and curving balconies summon up a Hollywood fantasy of the good life. Tawny wood inlays, burnished natural leathers are contrasted with chrome, mirrors and crystal with a maroon-blue deco pattern rug beneath. It is a stage set, to be sure, but it is also a serene, noble space.

The great inside auditorium, with its "sunburst" set of curving plaster arches, is the city's largest movie theater. The interiors were designed by Edward Durell Stone, who in his art deco days was an employee of Wallace K. Harrison, one of the many architects involved in the Rockefeller Center complex—still the finest skyscraper grouping in the nation.

RADIO CITY MUSIC HALL

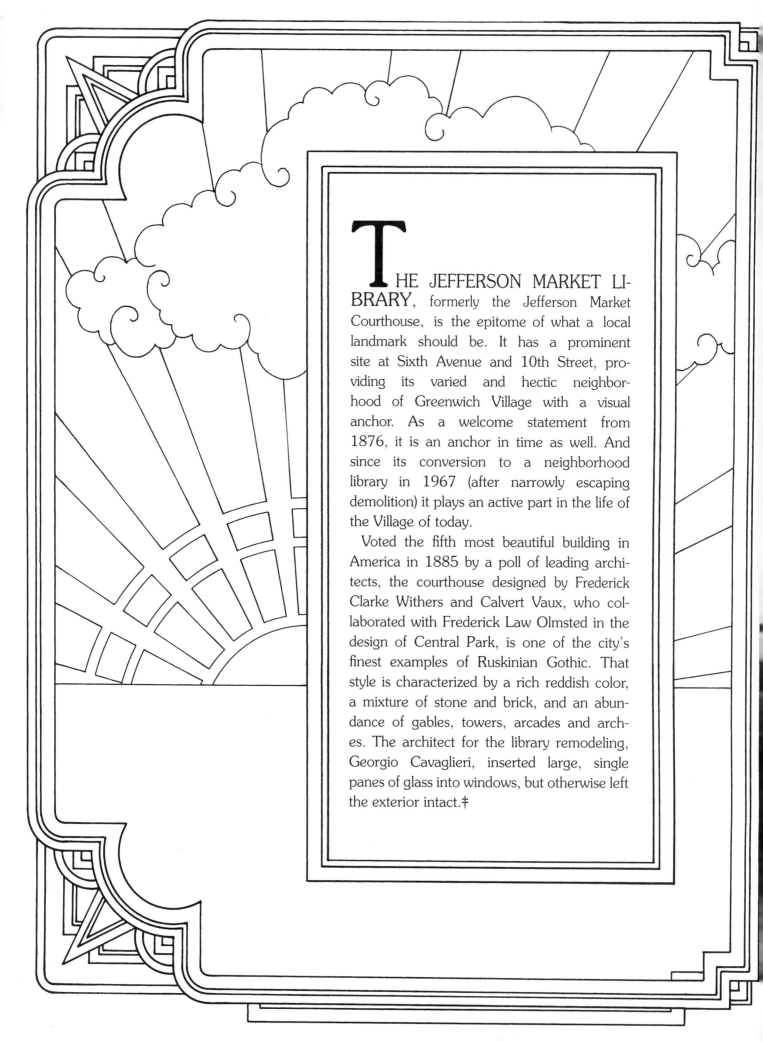

THE JEFFERSON MARKET LIBRARY, formerly the Jefferson Market Courthouse, is the epitome of what a local landmark should be. It has a prominent site at Sixth Avenue and 10th Street, providing its varied and hectic neighborhood of Greenwich Village with a visual anchor. As a welcome statement from 1876, it is an anchor in time as well. And since its conversion to a neighborhood library in 1967 (after narrowly escaping demolition) it plays an active part in the life of the Village of today.

Voted the fifth most beautiful building in America in 1885 by a poll of leading architects, the courthouse designed by Frederick Clarke Withers and Calvert Vaux, who collaborated with Frederick Law Olmsted in the design of Central Park, is one of the city's finest examples of Ruskinian Gothic. That style is characterized by a rich reddish color, a mixture of stone and brick, and an abundance of gables, towers, arcades and arches. The architect for the library remodeling, Georgio Cavaglieri, inserted large, single panes of glass into windows, but otherwise left the exterior intact.‡

JEFFERSON MARKET LIBRARY

S

ST. THOMAS CHURCH on Fifth Avenue at 53rd Street, completed in 1914, is one of the most creative of the city's many 20th-century interpretations of the Gothic style. There was no model for St. Thomas—it is in every way a building of its time, like the Woolworth Tower employing Gothic elements in the service of a new building program.

The intent was to give New York an urban Gothic church—a church that would stand not in the countryside like English cathedrals, or in a village square as in France, but right on a city street. St. Thomas is not symmetrical: the heavy tower on the left side of its façade exists to anchor the church on its corner site and act as a pivot around that corner. The building's urbanistic role, in other words, is to turn the corner.

The church was designed by Cram, Goodhue and Ferguson. Cram was confirmed traditional Gothicist, and Goodhue a more eclectic designer who designed the famous reredos, the elaborate sculpture above the altar.†

ST. THOMAS' CHURCH

WATERSIDE, a mixed-income housing complex by Davis, Brody and Associates, was completed in 1973. In a city of generally mediocre publicly-assisted housing, it stands out as a thoughtful exercise in form and site-planning. The towers, which widen instead of narrow toward the top, are of square, clay-brown colored brick. They are an elegant variation on the standard slab, and are most notable for their chamfered (cut off) corners and projections instead of the dull setbacks on high floors of more mundane apartment buildings.

The four towers of Waterside are set on a platform in the East River above 23rd Street, carefully arranged to maximize both city and river views. There is a welcome amount of open space around the building (although it is unfortunately only minimally landscaped), and a pleasant riverfront promenade.

The architects have used the Waterside scheme as a loose model for other housing of their design in the city, and even in the short time since the project's completion it has greatly influenced housing designs by other architects.

WATERSIDE APARTMENTS

Now that Pennsylvania Station is gone, Grand Central Terminal is surely New York's major interior space. Splitting Park Avenue at 42nd Street, the building is a byword for the bustle of a great city as well as a brilliant combination of architecture, engineering, and urbanism. The innovative overall concept, which separates vehicular, pedestrian, train, and subway traffic was the work of Reed and Stem, a St. Paul firm, while Warren and Wetmore, the distinguished New York firm of Beaux Arts architects, assisted in the design of the building itself.

The fine Beaux Arts façade with its arched windows, doubled columns and sculptural centerpiece, had no model. It was a creative assemblage of design elements in the best historicist tradition. When it was completed in 1913, the stone façade was white; today, years of city soot have turned it a dreary gray.

There are plans for an office tower atop the terminal which would involve the demolition of the façade. This prospect is being fought in court by the city's Landmark Preservation Commission and a group of concerned citizens working to preserve the terminal—which, as designed, is all an entrance to a great city should be.†

GRAND CENTRAL TERMINAL

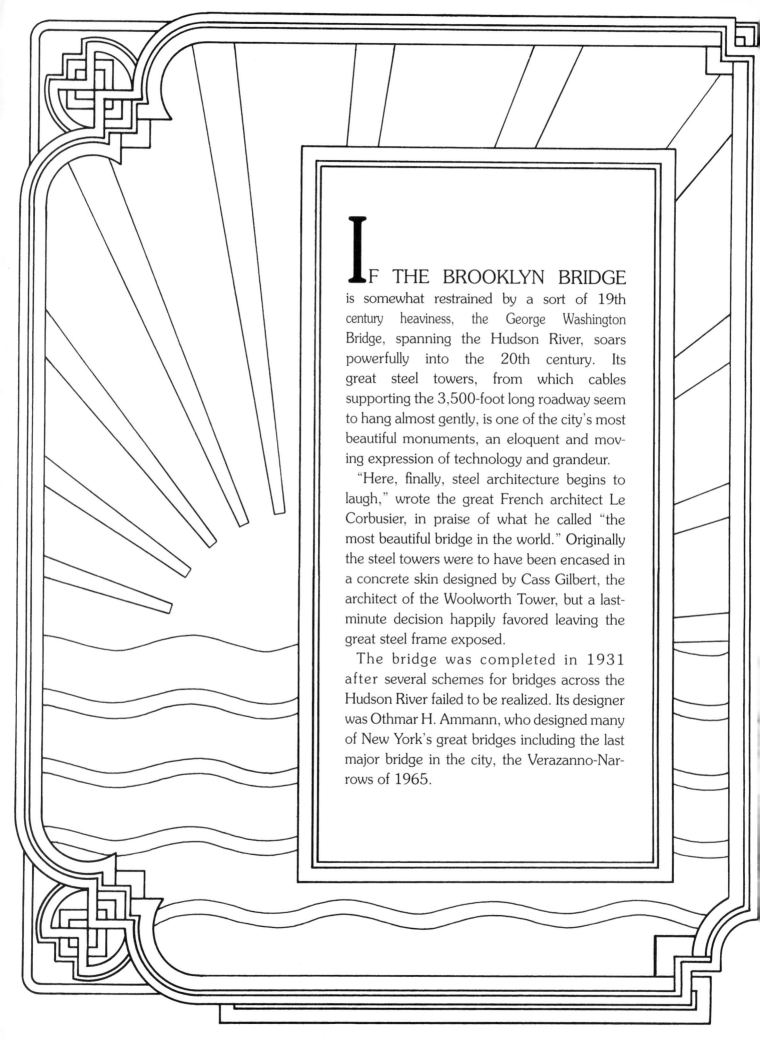

IF THE BROOKLYN BRIDGE is somewhat restrained by a sort of 19th century heaviness, the George Washington Bridge, spanning the Hudson River, soars powerfully into the 20th century. Its great steel towers, from which cables supporting the 3,500-foot long roadway seem to hang almost gently, is one of the city's most beautiful monuments, an eloquent and moving expression of technology and grandeur.

"Here, finally, steel architecture begins to laugh," wrote the great French architect Le Corbusier, in praise of what he called "the most beautiful bridge in the world." Originally the steel towers were to have been encased in a concrete skin designed by Cass Gilbert, the architect of the Woolworth Tower, but a last-minute decision happily favored leaving the great steel frame exposed.

The bridge was completed in 1931 after several schemes for bridges across the Hudson River failed to be realized. Its designer was Othmar H. Ammann, who designed many of New York's great bridges including the last major bridge in the city, the Verazanno-Narrows of 1965.

GEORGE WASHINGTON BRIDGE

THE BETHESDA FOUNTAIN

is an anomaly in Central Park—the most formal spot in an otherwise almost entirely rural landscape. Designed by Frederick Law Olmsted, the father of American landscape architecture, and Calvert Vaux, the park was constructed during the eighteen-sixties and eighteen-seventies over what had been a squalid, swampy site. Olmsted and Vaux's goal was to provide a place where the classes could mingle in the democratic spirit. With the interests in mind of New Yorkers who could never afford to leave the city, they provided a wide variety of different landscape experiences. Every part of the park—from woods to lakes to open meadows—was artificially created.

The fountain, centerpiece of the Terrace overlooking the Lake, was designed by Jacob Wrey Mould. The Angel of the Waters is the central figure.

Visible beyond the trees are the twin towers of one of the greatest of the Central Park West apartment houses, the San Remo, completed in 1930 to the designs of Emery Roth.†

BETHESDA FOUNTAIN

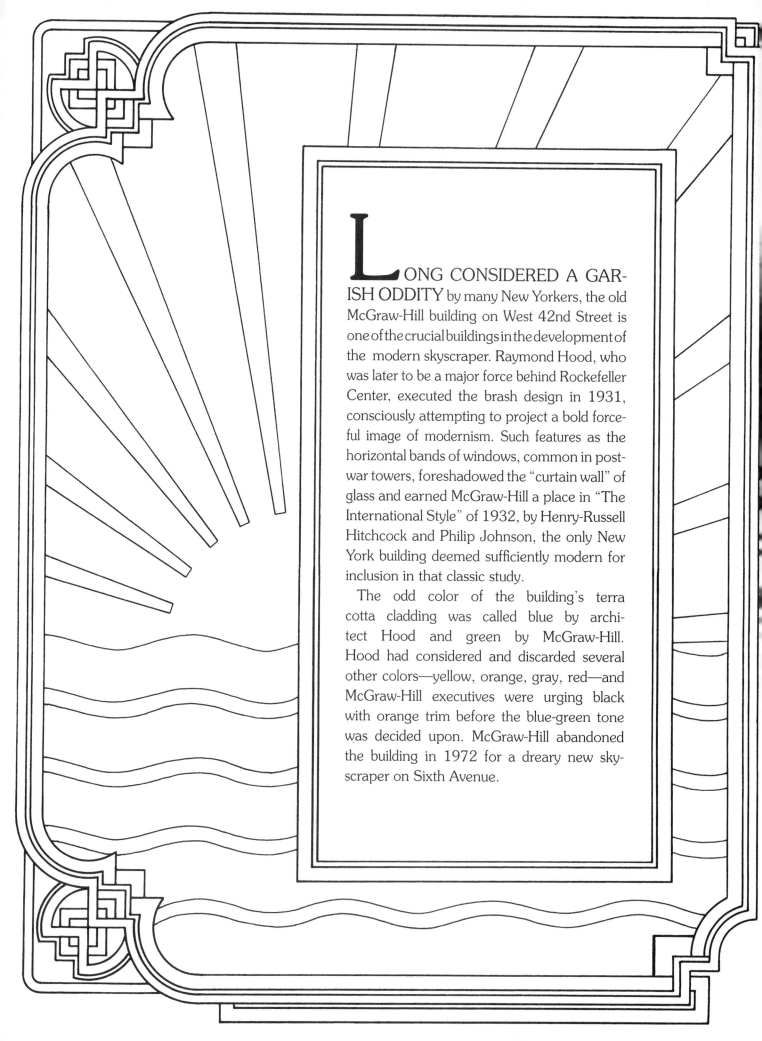

Long CONSIDERED A GAR-
ISH ODDITY by many New Yorkers, the old
McGraw-Hill building on West 42nd Street is
one of the crucial buildings in the development of
the modern skyscraper. Raymond Hood, who
was later to be a major force behind Rockefeller
Center, executed the brash design in 1931,
consciously attempting to project a bold force-
ful image of modernism. Such features as the
horizontal bands of windows, common in postwar towers, foreshadowed the "curtain wall" of
glass and earned McGraw-Hill a place in "The
International Style" of 1932, by Henry-Russell
Hitchcock and Philip Johnson, the only New
York building deemed sufficiently modern for
inclusion in that classic study.

The odd color of the building's terra
cotta cladding was called blue by architect Hood and green by McGraw-Hill.
Hood had considered and discarded several
other colors—yellow, orange, gray, red—and
McGraw-Hill executives were urging black
with orange trim before the blue-green tone
was decided upon. McGraw-Hill abandoned
the building in 1972 for a dreary new skyscraper on Sixth Avenue.

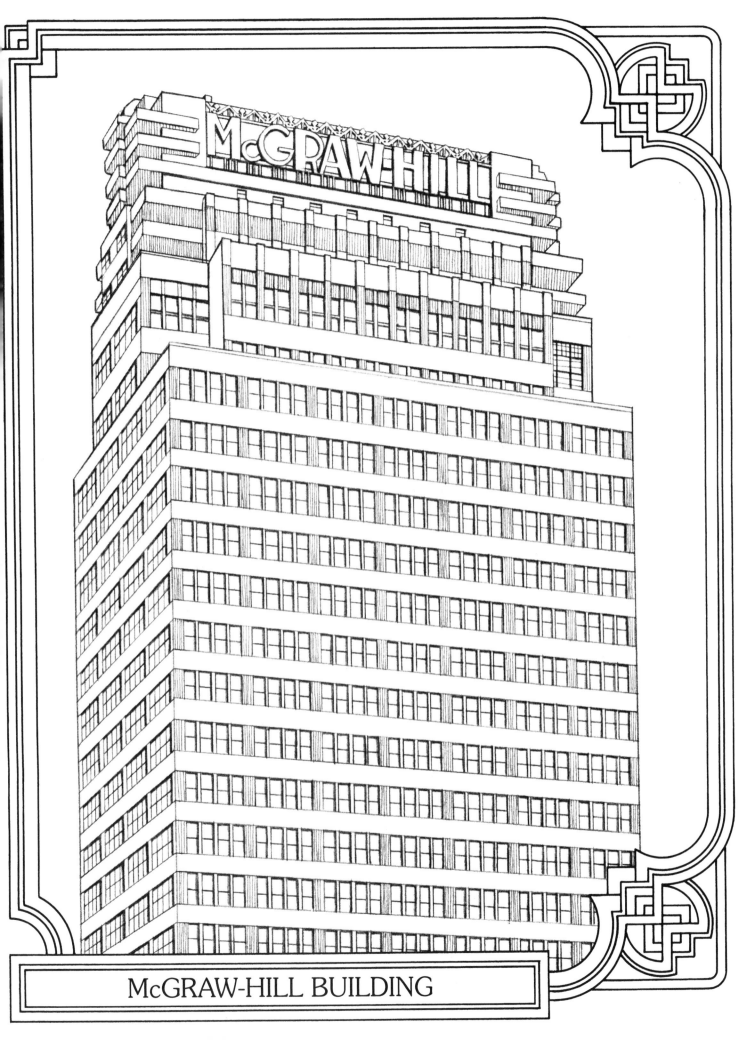

McGRAW-HILL BUILDING

THE STATUE OF LIBERTY has lifted her "lamp beside the golden door," in the words of Emma Lazarus's famous poem, since 1886, when she arrived in New York harbor as a gift from the people of France to America.

The 151-foot high, green-weathered statue is made of copper sheets welded together on a steel and iron frame. It was sculpted by Frederic Auguste Bartholdi in Paris, and shipped to the United States in sections. The base, which was designed by New York architect Richard Morris Hunt, was paid for by funds raised in a nationwide campaign. The engineering was the work of Gustave Eiffel, designer of the Eiffel Tower, who designed the lightweight framing system which supports the statue.

The Statue of Liberty is one of the world's great tourist attractions, and guidebooks are filled with such information as the length of Liberty's index finger (8 feet). But far more important is the statue's role as a monument to the day when hundreds of thousands of immigrants passed by her gaze to enter the port of New York—for all of them the gateway to America, and to a new life.

STATUE OF LIBERTY

L OUIS SULLIVAN, the great Chicago architect who more than any other gave modern form to the skyscraper and tried to break it away from historicist imitation, did most of his work in the Midwest. But his one building in New York, the 1898 Bayard Building on Bleecker Street east of Broadway, is among his best.

The 12-story building is elaborately ornamented, but as in most of Sullivan's work the ornament exists to emphasize the structure, not to obscure it. As a result, the supporting piers of the building are wide and heavy; in between them, Sullivan shows by his use of a narrow strip that he is only dividing the windows, not providing structural support.

The ground floor of the building, which was originally the Condict Building, has been altered, but the rest of the elaborate façade remains intact. The six angels below the cornice were not the choice of Sullivan, who rarely used human figures in his ornament, but were included at the request of the original client, Silas Condict.†

BAYARD BUILDING

ITS HEIGHT HAD BEEN SUR-
PASSED by the World Trade Center, but
no matter: the Empire State Building never
really had to rely on its "tallest building" title
for status. Height aside, it has always been
a splendid piece of architecture on its own
terms.

Opened in 1931 at the bottom of the de-
pression, and designed by Shreve, Lamb and
Harmon, the building is located at Fifth Avenue
and 34th Street, once the site of the Waldorf-
Astoria. Unlike many skyscrapers, it works
well in its urban context. The heavy base on
which it sits comes out to the street, hiding the
height of the tower and thus avoiding the tre-
mendous sense of weight generated by sheer
slabs like the World Trade Center.

But the Empire State Building is perhaps
most successful as image. The profile of its
gray chrome, ornamented spire, distinctive
and majestically recognizable without being
flamboyant, has become a virtual trademark
of New York.

EMPIRE STATE BUILDING

NEW YORK'S MAYORS still occupy the same quarters built for city government in 1812. City Hall, an elegant mixture of French Renaissance and Federal styles, was the work of Joseph Mangin, a Frenchman, and John McComb Jr., a New Yorker, who won a $350 prize in competition for a design for a new seat of government for the city.

The building was originally of marble, but its delicate, precise façade was restored in limestone in 1959. Inside, City Hall's rotunda contains a graceful double staircase of marble and several splendid hearing rooms.

The city's bureaucracy long ago outgrew City Hall and the Municipal Building of 1914 by McKim, Mead and White was its attempt to provide for future growth. The 32-story granite structure behind City Hall remains one of the city's best early skyscrapers. A noble exercise in the free and creative use of classical, largely Roman, details, the power of the building's great arch straddling Chambers Street sets an example of good urban relations. A recent cleaning restored it to its original white color.†

CITY HALL & MUNICIPAL BUILDING

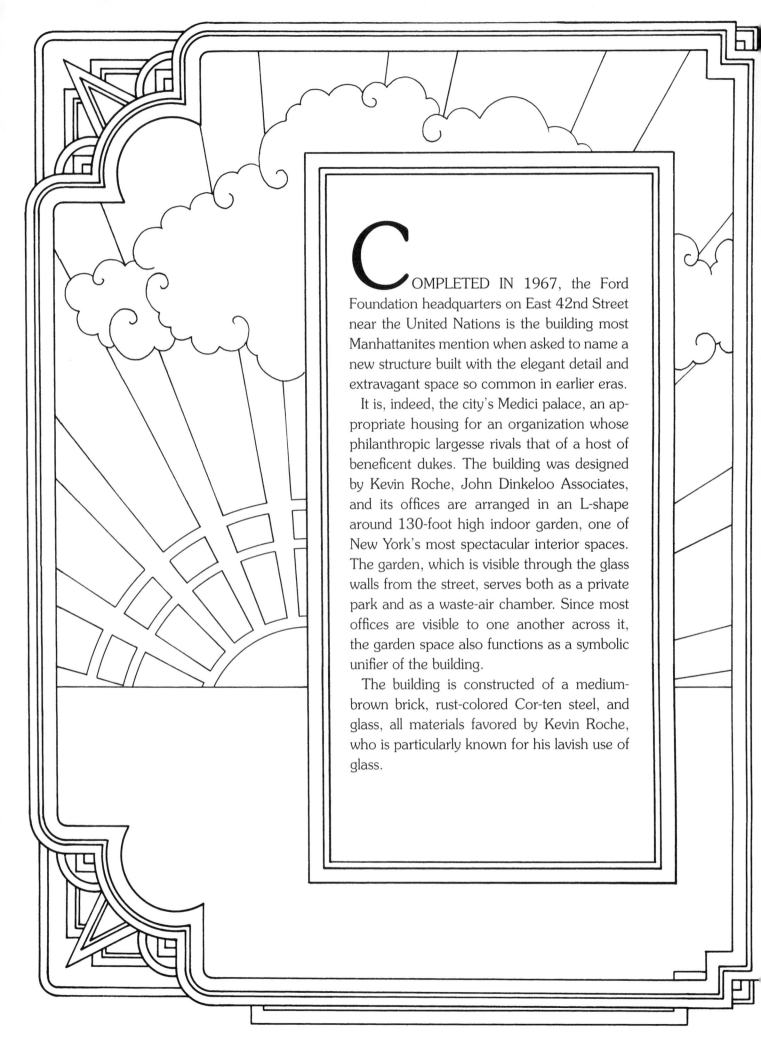

COMPLETED IN 1967, the Ford Foundation headquarters on East 42nd Street near the United Nations is the building most Manhattanites mention when asked to name a new structure built with the elegant detail and extravagant space so common in earlier eras.

It is, indeed, the city's Medici palace, an appropriate housing for an organization whose philanthropic largesse rivals that of a host of beneficent dukes. The building was designed by Kevin Roche, John Dinkeloo Associates, and its offices are arranged in an L-shape around 130-foot high indoor garden, one of New York's most spectacular interior spaces. The garden, which is visible through the glass walls from the street, serves both as a private park and as a waste-air chamber. Since most offices are visible to one another across it, the garden space also functions as a symbolic unifier of the building.

The building is constructed of a medium-brown brick, rust-colored Cor-ten steel, and glass, all materials favored by Kevin Roche, who is particularly known for his lavish use of glass.

FORD FOUNDATION

FRANK LLOYD WRIGHT rarely admitted to liking any building not his own, much less an old one, but he dearly loved The Plaza. Of course, so has almost everyone who ever passed the corner of Fifth Avenue and 59th Street, where the gracious, wildly exaggerated white-brick French Renaissance chateau with its green copper roof has stood since 1907. It is as mingled with the lore of New York as Grand Central Terminal or the Empire State Building, and perhaps inspires more affection than any other monument in New York.

The building was designed by Henry Hardenbergh, who two decades earlier had designed the Dakota. With The Plaza, Hardenbergh achieved a kind of controlled exuberance, a warmth and elegance without too much ostentation. The public rooms, most notably the majestic Oak Room, are dignified and welcoming without the touch of silliness found in less disciplined examples of Beaux Arts design of the period.

The Plaza closed on April 30, 2005 to undergo extensive renovations and restoration. It reopened in the winter of 2007-08 and offers 130 hotel rooms plus 152 private condo hotel units.†

PLAZA HOTEL

THE BROOKLYN BRIDGE spanning the East River is a triumph of art and engineering. Completed in 1883, it was the longest suspension bridge in the world, and the most majestic, soaring structure in a city that had barely begun to build the skyscraper.

The bridge was designed by John A. Roebling, who died just before construction began in 1867. Roebling's son, Washington A. Roebling, who was himself injured in construction 1872, spent eleven years supervising the work on the bridge from his house in Brooklyn Heights.

The bridge's Gothic masonry towers are not as light as those of more recent bridges, but the weblike pattern of its steel cables has a grace that has never been equaled.

No single structure may ever equal the bridge in terms of the impact it has had on the city. "All modern New York, heroic New York," Kenneth Clark, the art historian, has said, "started with the Brooklyn Bridge."†

SKYLINE & BROOKLYN BRIDGE

MANY OF NEW YORK'S SKYSCRAPERS are dismissed as cold and austere. But that charge has never been leveled against the Chrysler Building, the 1930 tower that reigned for a few brief months, until the Empire State Building's completion, as the tallest building in the world.

Chrysler's flamboyant spire, a series of stainless-steel arches with triangular window openings, perfectly realizes the romantic attempt to symbolize the machine age that was the essence of art deco design. The building also sports gargoyles modeled after automobile radiator daps and elaborate basketweave and Aztec-inspired ornaments. The mélange was once dismissed as foolish romanticism by serious modernists; now, thanks to the recent wave of interest in art deco, Chrysler has become one of the city's treasured icons, and its architect, William Van Alen, a resurrected hero.

The African marble-and-chrome lobby remains intact, a perfect setting for the nineteen-thirties vision of the machine-age city that the building represents.

CHRYSLER BUILDING

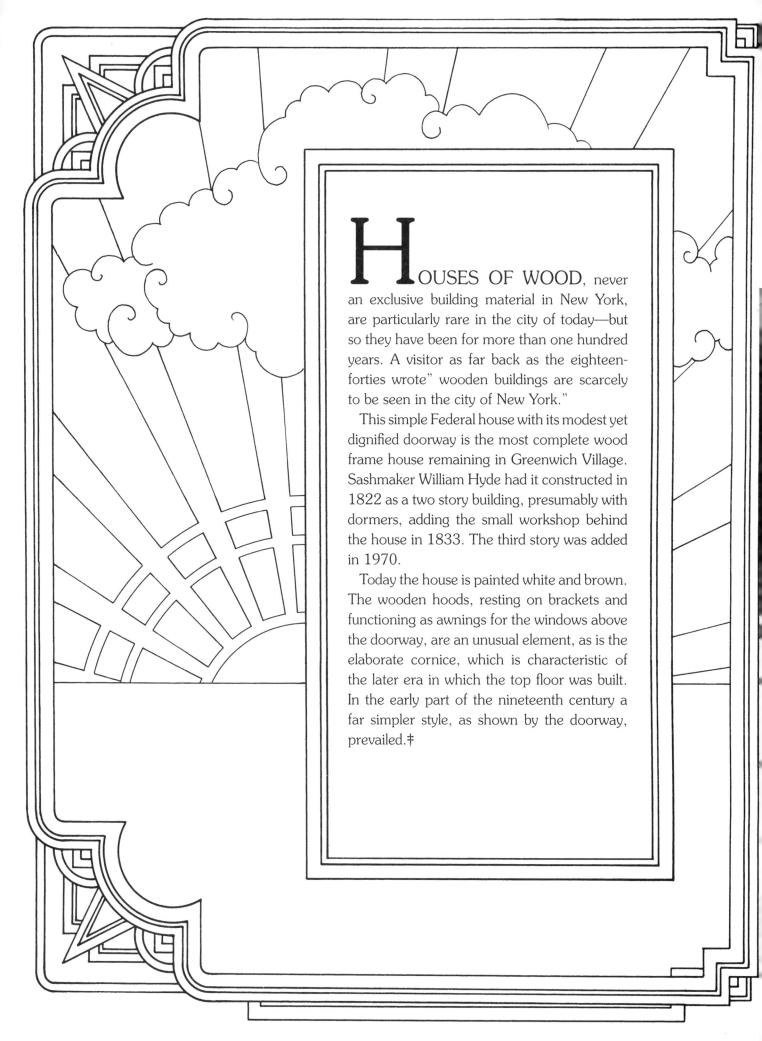

Houses of Wood

Houses of wood, never an exclusive building material in New York, are particularly rare in the city of today—but so they have been for more than one hundred years. A visitor as far back as the eighteen-forties wrote" wooden buildings are scarcely to be seen in the city of New York."

This simple Federal house with its modest yet dignified doorway is the most complete wood frame house remaining in Greenwich Village. Sashmaker William Hyde had it constructed in 1822 as a two story building, presumably with dormers, adding the small workshop behind the house in 1833. The third story was added in 1970.

Today the house is painted white and brown. The wooden hoods, resting on brackets and functioning as awnings for the windows above the doorway, are an unusual element, as is the elaborate cornice, which is characteristic of the later era in which the top floor was built. In the early part of the nineteenth century a far simpler style, as shown by the doorway, prevailed.‡

17 GROVE STREET

THE GRAY STONE ARCH AT WASHINGTON SQUARE is the symbolic center of Greenwich Village—although its location in Washington Square Park at the bottom of Fifth Avenue puts it somewhat east of the Village's real geographic center. The present arch, a permanent version dating from 1889-92, replaced a wooden arch created by McKim, Mead and White in 1876 to celebrate the Centennial of the American Revolution. It is Manhattan's only formal arch. (While Manhattanites rarely admit to being outdone by Brooklyn, a far grander arch exists there at Grand Army Plaza.)

On the north side of Washington Square is one of the city's few surviving rows of Greek Revival townhouses. In the eighteen-thirties such houses surrounded the square, which for years was among the city's most exclusive addresses and the setting for innumerable scenes from the novels of Edith Wharton and Henry James. The buildings to the east of Fifth Avenue are facades only; the insides were gutted and turned into apartments. Most of the western end of the row, parts of which were designed by the leading Greek Revival architects A. J. Davies, Ithiel Town and Martin Thompson, remains.

LET US RAISE A STANDARD TO WHICH THE WISE
AND THE HONEST CAN REPAIR " THE EVENT
IS IN THE HANDS OF GOD ★ WASHINGTON

WASHINGTON SQUARE ARCH

THE INDUSTRIAL LANDSCAPE often provides striking, if inadvertent, architectural monuments, of which the grain elevators across the Midwest are an outstanding example. Perhaps New York's best version of such an unintentional memorable architectural statement is the Municipal Asphalt Plant on the East River Drive at 91st Street.

The plant was built in 1944 to the designs of Kahn and Jacobs, and like the grain elevators, is a simple functional form that in its plainness takes on a certain monumentality. Here the shape is a huge arch, and the entire building consists simply of exposed concrete set over the steel arch frame. The shape reflects the form of the machinery within; this logical relationship made the building particularly attractive to avant-garde critics of the nineteen-forties, who hailed it as one of New York's most important statements in modernism.

The asphalt plant ceased operation in 1968. In 1984 this landmark building was converted into a recreation center, the Murphy Center at Asphalt Green.

MUNICIPAL ASPHALT PLANT

FEDERAL HALL NATIONAL MEMORIAL,

on Wall and Nassau Streets in the heart of the financial district is one of the city's finest examples of Greek Revival architecture. Designed by Ithiel Town and A. J. Davis, a prominent 19th-century firm, with John Frazee and Samuel Thompson, its strong colonnade of marble Doric columns is a powerful presence in the Wall Street area—and an interesting counterpoint to the 20th-century Greek temple front pasted onto the façade of the New York Stock Exchange across the street.

Built between 1834 and 1842 on the site of the original Federal Hall where George Washington took the oath of office in 1789, the building originally housed the Customs Service and later the U.S. Subtreasury. It is now a national monument, and its recently restored rotunda contains a federal museum. The building's back is on Pine Street; there is another Doric front on Wall Street, with a statue of George Washington on its majestic stairway.†

FEDERAL HALL NATIONAL MEMORIAL

THE ROW HOUSE is the essence of New York, as much as any of the city's great monuments. Few row houses are great pieces of architecture in themselves, but many built in the nineteenth and early twentieth centuries are well-crafted and finely detailed examples of townhouse design which are a significant motif in the fabric of the city.

By mid-century the Italianate brownstone was most common, and the term brownstone has come to be generic for all row houses. Late in the century the Romanesque style predominated, as exemplified by these excellent houses on West 82nd Street.

Built of brick and stone around the eighteeneighties, a time when the West Side was becoming fashionable as an upper middle class area, their bay windows and large stoops are typical of the houses of the period, although their details are somewhat more restrained than many of the West Side houses. Along with other New York row house areas, the West Side is enjoying a renaissance, as deteriorated houses are restored by residents who elect to live in the city instead of the suburbs.

ROMANESQUE BROWNSTONES

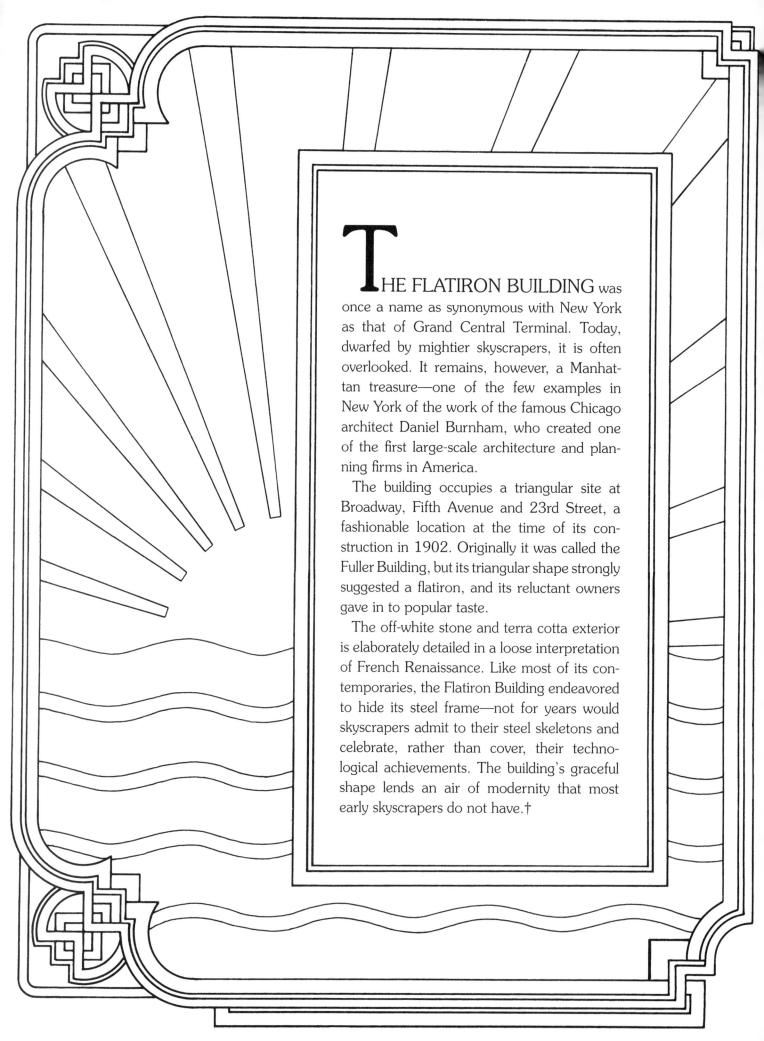

THE FLATIRON BUILDING was once a name as synonymous with New York as that of Grand Central Terminal. Today, dwarfed by mightier skyscrapers, it is often overlooked. It remains, however, a Manhattan treasure—one of the few examples in New York of the work of the famous Chicago architect Daniel Burnham, who created one of the first large-scale architecture and planning firms in America.

The building occupies a triangular site at Broadway, Fifth Avenue and 23rd Street, a fashionable location at the time of its construction in 1902. Originally it was called the Fuller Building, but its triangular shape strongly suggested a flatiron, and its reluctant owners gave in to popular taste.

The off-white stone and terra cotta exterior is elaborately detailed in a loose interpretation of French Renaissance. Like most of its contemporaries, the Flatiron Building endeavored to hide its steel frame—not for years would skyscrapers admit to their steel skeletons and celebrate, rather than cover, their technological achievements. The building's graceful shape lends an air of modernity that most early skyscrapers do not have.†

FLATIRON BUILDING

LEVER HOUSE, completed in 1952, influenced a generation of postwar skyscrapers both in New York and elsewhere. It was the second all-glass "curtain wall" skyscraper to be built in New York (the United Nations Secretariat was the first), and it led the way for the rebuilding of lower Park Avenue in its image.

The building was one of the first major works of Gordon Bunshaft of Skidmore, Owings and Merrill, who went on to become a major force in American postwar modernism. Its two slabs, one upright and one used as the base, do not occupy the maximum amount of space permitted by the zoning law, but leave a significant amount of open space. This space, on the open ground floor, is accessible to the public. The rest is pure volume beside the tower slab.

This green-glass building was hailed in its time and remains a classic. Recent critics, however, have questioned the decision to leave the ground floor empty, which makes it somewhat lifeless, and the placement of the tower perpendicular to Park Avenue, which cuts a hole in the celebrated "street wall" of the Avenue.

LEVER HOUSE

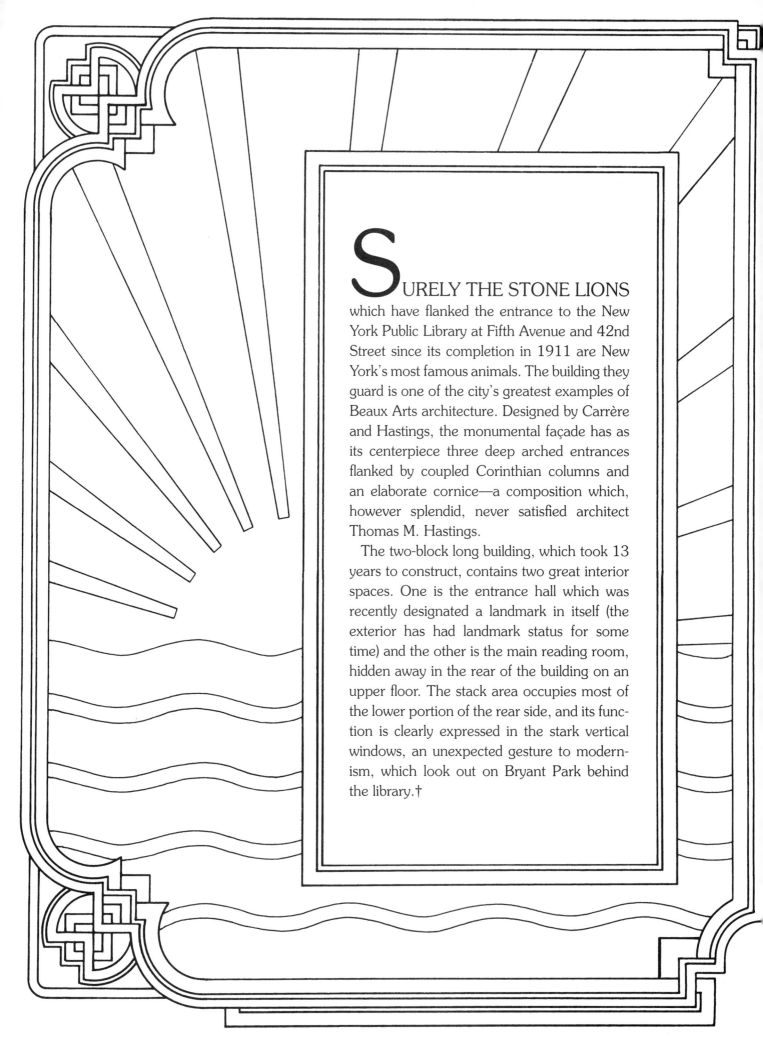

S URELY THE STONE LIONS

which have flanked the entrance to the New York Public Library at Fifth Avenue and 42nd Street since its completion in 1911 are New York's most famous animals. The building they guard is one of the city's greatest examples of Beaux Arts architecture. Designed by Carrère and Hastings, the monumental façade has as its centerpiece three deep arched entrances flanked by coupled Corinthian columns and an elaborate cornice—a composition which, however splendid, never satisfied architect Thomas M. Hastings.

The two-block long building, which took 13 years to construct, contains two great interior spaces. One is the entrance hall which was recently designated a landmark in itself (the exterior has had landmark status for some time) and the other is the main reading room, hidden away in the rear of the building on an upper floor. The stack area occupies most of the lower portion of the rear side, and its function is clearly expressed in the stark vertical windows, an unexpected gesture to modernism, which look out on Bryant Park behind the library.†

NEW YORK PUBLIC LIBRARY

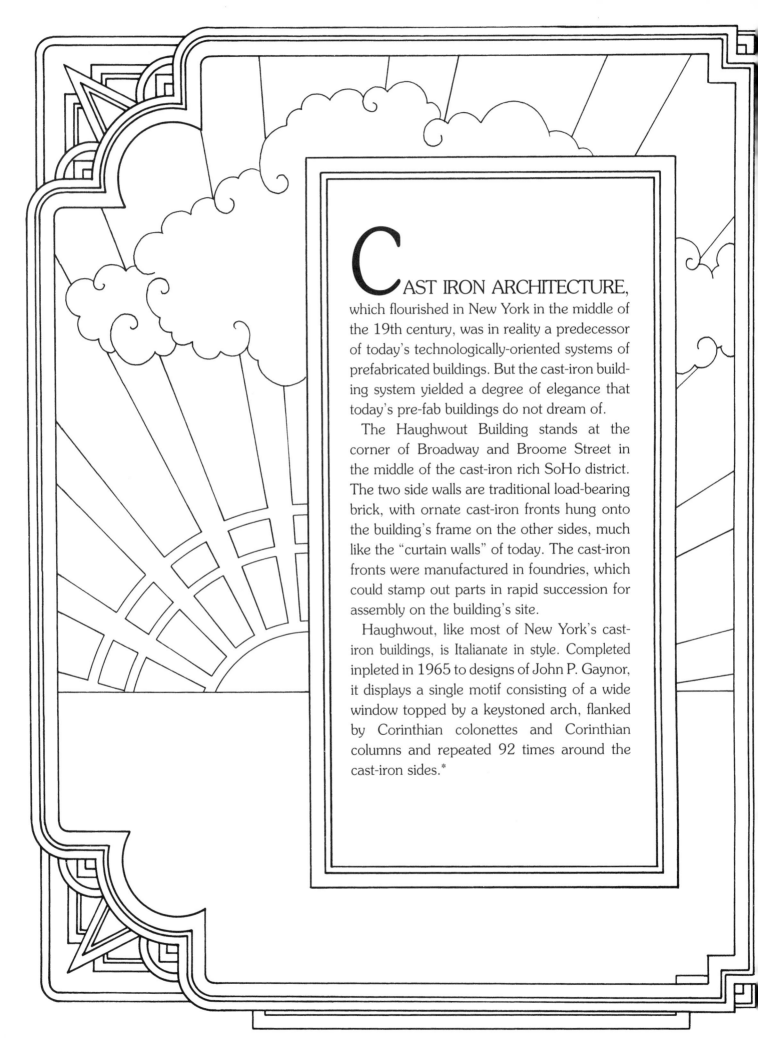

Cast Iron Architecture,

which flourished in New York in the middle of the 19th century, was in reality a predecessor of today's technologically-oriented systems of prefabricated buildings. But the cast-iron building system yielded a degree of elegance that today's pre-fab buildings do not dream of.

The Haughwout Building stands at the corner of Broadway and Broome Street in the middle of the cast-iron rich SoHo district. The two side walls are traditional load-bearing brick, with ornate cast-iron fronts hung onto the building's frame on the other sides, much like the "curtain walls" of today. The cast-iron fronts were manufactured in foundries, which could stamp out parts in rapid succession for assembly on the building's site.

Haughwout, like most of New York's cast-iron buildings, is Italianate in style. Completed inpleted in 1965 to designs of John P. Gaynor, it displays a single motif consisting of a wide window topped by a keystoned arch, flanked by Corinthian colonettes and Corinthian columns and repeated 92 times around the cast-iron sides.*

HAUGHWOUT BUILDING

THE NEW YORK YACHT CLUB, completed in 1899, is generally considered Beaux-Arts in style, but it is too original—not to mention exuberant—to be restrained by the limits of any stylistic category.

The architects were Warren and Wetmore, a prominent and eclectic New York firm which later worked on Grand Central Terminal. They used windows shaped like the sterns of eighteenth century Dutch sailing ships as the main motif of the elaborately ornamented façade of white limestone. The nautical type windows are set neatly into larger windows and a row of columns which proclaim the building's grand scale, anchoring it to the streetscape of West 44th Street between Fifth and Sixth Avenues, a better-than-average midtown block which also contains the Harvard Club and the Algonquin Hotel. As with most of the city's great clubhouses, the Yacht Club has one majestic space within—in this case used for the display of ship models.

NEW YORK YACHT CLUB

THE VILLARD HOUSES are perhaps the city's finest surviving townhouse grouping, and one of the earliest achievements of the architectural firm that more than any other left is mark on turn-of-the-century New York—McKim, Mead and White.

The brownstone townhouses, which stand on Madison Avenue between 50th and 51st Streets, form a U-shape around a courtyard originally used as a carriage turn-around. They date from 1882-86 and are among the city's earliest examples of the Italian Renaissance style.

Henry Villard, the owner of the New York Evening Post, commissioned the grouping. One of the houses was the headquarters of Random House, the publishers, for many years, before becoming the property of the Roman Catholic Archdiocese of New York. During the 1970's the complex was threatened with demolition, but instead, the houses were incorporated into the Palace Hotel.†

HENRY VILLARD HOUSES

THE DAKOTA, completed in 1884, is the early masterpiece of Henry Janeway Hardenbergh, later the architect of the Plaza Hotel. Its heavy, German Renaissance forms and elegant proportions have made it for generations a landmark on Central Park West at 72nd Street.

The building was one of the first attempts to persuade well-to-do New Yorkers to live in apartment houses, which in the 19th century were still associated with the working classes. The enormous rooms, high ceilings and elaborate paneling and interior detailing were all a conscious effort to convince tenants that they were not moving down to a tenement but up into a more elegant world.

Threatened with demolition around 1960, the yellow brick building was saved when its tenants, (many of whom are prominent in the arts), purchased it and turned it into a cooperative. The unusual name began as a joke; in 1880, when construction started, the area was barely built up, and New Yorkers asked builder Edward S. Clark why he didn't go slightly farther out and build his building "in the Dakota territory."†

DAKOTA APARTMENTS

FRANK LLOYD WRIGHT'S GUG-GENHEIM MUSEUM is most notable as an interior space. Its rounded white form, like so much of the architect's late work (it was completed in 1959, the year of Wright's death) pays little heed to what is around it, and in the hands of a lesser architect would have done real damage to the harmony of upper Fifth Avenue. As it is, the building is an eccentric that has made a comfortable peace with its staid surroundings.

The inside, however, is one of New York's architectural triumphs—a great round hall, with galleries spiraling up the side, all topped by an elaborate glass dome. Wright, a master of the processional element, wisely used a low-ceilinged entrance. Beyond the vestibule the space suddenly shoots up to its full height, and affords the viewer one of the city's great spatial experiences.

GUGGENHEIM MUSEUM

U NTIL THE CHRYSLER
BUILDING rose to challenge it, the Woolworth Tower was the world's tallest building. And like the Chrysler Building, the Woolworth Tower was more than just a record holder.

The 792-foot tall building, opened in 1913, is the best-known work of the architect Cass Gilbert, a skillful American historicist designer, one of a group that rejected modernism and reinterpreted historical styles in modern contexts. Gilbert here used a loose version of Gothic architecture reportedly at the request of builder Frank Woolworth, the dime-store magnate. At the time of Woolworth's construction, architects were grappling to find a style appropriate to the new form of the skyscraper, and while the use of Gothic was not welcomed by avant-garde designers, it was rationalized on the basis of the appropriately strong vertical lines.

The building rises to 60 stories with extraordinary grace: Woolworth indeed remains New York's greatest pre-World War I skyscraper, and its three story arcaded entrance lobby, with murals, glass mosaics and bas-reliefs of the architect, builder, and owner, happily remains intact.

WOOLWORTH TOWER

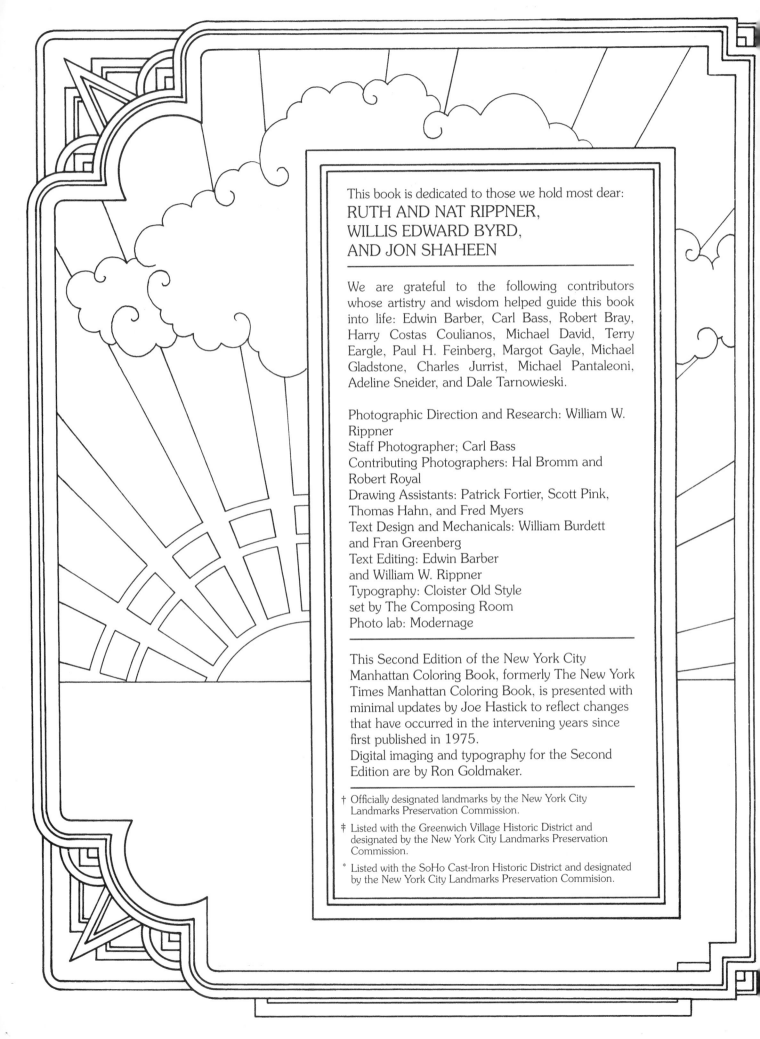

This book is dedicated to those we hold most dear:
RUTH AND NAT RIPPNER,
WILLIS EDWARD BYRD,
AND JON SHAHEEN

We are grateful to the following contributors whose artistry and wisdom helped guide this book into life: Edwin Barber, Carl Bass, Robert Bray, Harry Costas Coulianos, Michael David, Terry Eargle, Paul H. Feinberg, Margot Gayle, Michael Gladstone, Charles Jurrist, Michael Pantaleoni, Adeline Sneider, and Dale Tarnowieski.

Photographic Direction and Research: William W. Rippner
Staff Photographer; Carl Bass
Contributing Photographers: Hal Bromm and Robert Royal
Drawing Assistants: Patrick Fortier, Scott Pink, Thomas Hahn, and Fred Myers
Text Design and Mechanicals: William Burdett and Fran Greenberg
Text Editing: Edwin Barber and William W. Rippner
Typography: Cloister Old Style set by The Composing Room
Photo lab: Modernage

This Second Edition of the New York City Manhattan Coloring Book, formerly The New York Times Manhattan Coloring Book, is presented with minimal updates by Joe Hastick to reflect changes that have occurred in the intervening years since first published in 1975.
Digital imaging and typography for the Second Edition are by Ron Goldmaker.

† Officially designated landmarks by the New York City Landmarks Preservation Commission.

‡ Listed with the Greenwich Village Historic District and designated by the New York City Landmarks Preservation Commission.

* Listed with the SoHo Cast-Iron Historic District and designated by the New York City Landmarks Preservation Commision.